SO-CEZ-405

If People Were Cats

OTHER BOOKS BY LEIGH W. RUTLEDGE

Diary of a Cat
A Cat's Little Instruction Book
Cat Love Letters
It Seemed Like a Good Idea at the Time
The Lefthander's Guide to Life
Excuses, Excuses

LEIGH W. RUTLEDGE

If People Were Cats

A DUTTON BOOK

DUTTON
Published by the Penguin Group
Penguin Books USA Inc., 375 Hudson Street, New York, New York 10014, U.S.A.
Penguin Books Ltd, 27 Wrights Lane, London W8 5TZ, England
Penguin Books Australia Ltd, Ringwood, Victoria, Australia
Penguin Books Canada Ltd, 10 Alcorn Avenue, Toronto, Ontario, Canada M4V 3B2
Penguin Books (N.Z.) Ltd, 182–190 Wairau Road, Auckland 10, New Zealand

Penguin Books Ltd, Registered Offices: Harmondsworth, Middlesex, England

First published by Dutton, an imprint of Dutton Signet,
a division of Penguin Books USA Inc.
Distributed in Canada by McClelland & Stewart Inc.

First Printing, April, 1997
1   3   5   7   9   10   8   6   4   2

Copyright © Leigh W. Rutledge, 1997
All rights reserved

 REGISTERED TRADEMARK—MARCA REGISTRADA

LIBRARY OF CONGRESS CATALOGING-IN-PUBLICATION DATA:
Rutledge, Leigh W.
If people were cats / Leigh W. Rutledge.
p.   cm.
ISBN 0-525-94276-9 (acid-free paper)
1. Cats—Poetry.   2. Humorous poetry, American.   I. Title.
PS3568.U8238138   1997
811'.54—dc20   96-41689
CIP

Printed in the United States of America
Set in Tekton and Freestyle Script
Designed by Eve L. Kirch

Without limiting the rights under copyright reserved above, no part of this publica-
tion may be reproduced, stored in or introduced into a retrieval system, or trans-
mitted, in any form, or by any means (electronic, mechanical, photocopying,
recording, or otherwise), without the prior written permission of both the copyright owner and the above publisher of this book.

This book is printed on acid-free paper.

This book is dedicated,
with love and devotion,
to all of my cats:
Amanda, Beardsley, Bobbie Boop,
Boo, Grouch, Kitterin,
Little Bull, Mabel, Maybelline,
Mrs. Moore, Perch, Peter Finn,
Sally, Shasta, Sissygambis,
Snowball, Spitfire, Tonya,
Twyla, and White Bear—
and all of the animals who have ever
graced me with their instructive presence
and their trust.

If People Were Cats

If people were cats,
From Shanghai to Bournemouth
The only fur coats
Would be ones
    You were born with.

———

If people were cats
The couch would be tattered,
The draperies shredded,
The knickknacks all shattered,
The mattress unmattressed,
The teacups all battered,
The shelved books unshelved,
The hat stand unhattered.
Every lamp would be broken
As if of no matter,
The blinds all in tangles,
The china unplattered,

The paintings at angles,
The flatware unflattered.
All night and all day
The fun never ceases,
'Til all in the house
Is lying in pieces.
The world unwhorled—
What ruin they're creating!
The country undone
By cat decorating.

———

*I*f people were cats
The hairdresser's job
Would not be to give you
A perm or a bob

Instead the salon
Is where you'd be seen
Having your hair
Licked wonderfully clean.

———

If people were cats
Your granny might be
Spending her Sundays
Up in a tree

First thing in the morning
She'd zoom to the top
Ignoring your pleas of
"Please, Granny, stop!"

High in the sky,
On a branch she would sway
'Til the firemen came
To take her away

Up goes the ladder
It's the end of her spree
The fifth granny that day
Brought down from a tree.

———

*I*f people were
        cats
No one would
        be
Embarrassed to
        stop
And sniff
        peonies.

Or cockscomb and
        cowslips
And sweet pussy
        willows;
They'd sleep in
        snapdragons
With violets as
        pillows.

Sniffing the dogwood
  and
Duckweed, they'd
  treat
Themselves to a
  flowering
Bon appétit—
      If people were cats
      That's what they'd eat.

Wolfbane and
      foxgloves
Carnations and
      jasmine
Larkspur and
      harebells
And, yes,
      dandelions.

If people were
            cats
What would you
            bet
They'd sneak in and
            steal
Some fresh baby's
            breath?

"As I came to
            work
This morning," they'd
            whisper,
"I devoured a
            tasty
Maroon lady's
            slipper!"

_____

If people were cats
A rat-tat-tat-tat
There'd be no guns
No, nothing like that

Instead the Congress
Would have to pass laws
Banning possession
    Of concealed claws

———

Need?
They
Floor
Whichever
to
Up
Way
Their
Clawing
Everyone
and
Carpet
in
Covered
Completely
Building
State
Empire
the
of
Outside
the
Imagine
You
Can

$\mathcal{S}$tart here

Martina and Chrissie play tennis, you know
The object's to knock
A small ball to and fro
But if they were cats
Just think of the shouts
When instead they caught
The ball in their mouths.

———

*I*f people were cats
   No one would care if you're orange
   No one would care if you're gray
Or white   Or black
   Or a parfait mix of the two
   No one would care if you have stripes
      Or spots
      Or are even missing your tail
   No one would care if you're brown
   No one would care if you're blue
Most of all, if you were a cat
   You'd be utterly content
      Just being you.

———

*T*o the dismay of every prude,
All sunbathing would be
nude,
If people were cats.

———

"If people were cats,"
Said the rabbi to me,
"I think I can say,
With fair certainty,
That we'd all be Jewish,
Don't you agree?
What's one thing that cats
Possess plentifully?
Chutzpah galore!
It's part of their creed.
Besides," he affirmed
Exuberantly,
"They're wanderers, too,
And as smart as can be.
I think I can say,
Self-evidently,
Cats as a tribe are
God's chosen species!"

"If people were cats,"
The bishop explained,
"Then we'd all be Catholics,
It's wholly ordained.
A cat's walk is silent,
Like monks in a nave,
But much more than that
There's our very name:
Catholics, Cat-holics,
Clearly proclaims
That cats and our faith
Are one and the same!
There's only one quandary
That I see ingrained
And that's how to keep
Our dogma restrained."

"If people were cats,"
The atheist cried,
"One look at the facts
Would doubtless decide
That cats have no need
For gods up on high.
They're too self-reliant,
And have too much pride.
Furthermore, any world
Where ticks and fleas dine
Would hardly be viewed
As created divine."

"Sshhh," said the Buddhist,
His voice like snowfall,
"If people were cats,
We'd be Buddhists all,
For of all of God's creatures
Lofty and small,
The cat is transported
Into rapt thrall
Meditating for hours
On specks on the wall."

———

*I*f people were cats,
Miss Manners would deem
It now *de rigueur*
To lick your plate clean.

What's more, she'd advise
Connoisseurs (*entre nous*)
It's perfectly fine
To lick others', too!

(And she'd no longer tell you to snub quick,
Someone nibbling his toenails in public.)

(Nor would she give you much heat
For scratching your ears with your feet.)

_____

IF PEOPLE WERE CATS THERE'D NEVER BE ANY USABLE TOILET PAPER IN THE HOUSE. EVERYONE'S IMPULSES TO PLAY WOULD CARRY THEM AWAY AND THE TOILET PAPER WOULD ALL BE UNRAVELED ALL OVER THE FLOOR EVERY DAY

If people were cats
Oh, what a curse!
To drag all about
And constantly nurse
Six kittens at once
On a bus or a train,
Six greedy kittens
Aboard an airplane,
Six hungry mouths,
All hungry at once,
Don't care if you're tired,
They're hungry for lunch—

Don't care where you are,
In traffic or sleeping,
Those six hungry mouths
Are hungry for feeding.
Mama's exhausted,
She doesn't complain,
She's hungry herself,
But has to abstain.
Better be careful or
Next year, my friend,
Six new hungry mouths
Will be at it again.

———

If people were cats,
    wars would last
    fifteen seconds (okay,
        maybe twenty—but only if catnip were involved),
    then everyone would curl up
    together
    on the sofa for a nice long nap.
Generals, formerly
    hissing and boxing each other's ears, would
    lick
    each other's foreheads clean instead.
That quiet purring you hear
    is soldiers, troops
    intertwined
    on a winter's night
    in the innocent promiscuity of peace.

After all, cats recognize what people
do not: that
anger, while real, is a fleeting
digression,
The heart's equivalent
of
a nasty furball.

———

*I*f people
     were cats,
There'd be holes
     in your hats,
But only just two,
Not one more
     than that.
Your hats
     would have holes,
Through which you'd cajole
Your two very big furry ears.

If people
        were cats,
There'd be holes
        in your pants,
But only just one,
(That's one more
        than none).
Your pants
        would have holes,
So you could unroll
Your tail that swings in the rear.

If people
    were cats,
There'd be holes
    in your masks.
How many, you ask?
    So many, I fear.
Your masks
    would have holes,
Through which you'd parole
All your lovely, protruding whiskers.

But even if you
Had holes
        in your hats,
And holes
        in your pants,
And holes
        in your masks,
And all of your clothes
        were as holesome as that,
You would be whole,
A well-clad wholesome cat,
Even if you
        had holes in your hats.

———

If people were cats,
     it would not be
          considered rude
               to drool

                    All over someone special
                    To show you think they're cool.

And while they slept,
     if you liked them best,
          to show them they are dear—

                    You'd purr upon their pillow
                    And drool right in their ear.

          _____

If people were cats,
I'm a believer—
Sex would be noisier,
And an awful lot briefer.

———

/f   n the air
                                                   i
    people   e
        were   s
            cats,   i
our rear ends would automatically r

Every time someone touched us
        on

        our lower backs anywhere.

                    _____

*O*h, if people cats could be,
Heed this simple platitude:
You and I would strut freely
Steeped in lordly cattitude.

Consolation take indeed:
Gentle purring fills us here
Rooms and gardens now softly
Imbued with calming catmosphere.

———

*I*f people were cats,
People would be Cats.

Gourmet
Every day: "Purr-fect
Squirrels Every Time."

Newsweek?
"Socks Speaks!" *National
Enquirer?* "Socks
Speaks in Tongues!" And *Seventeen*
(a hundred and two by cats'
reckoning): a magazine
for the aging.

———

*I*f people were cats, imagine strolling
upon a game of feline bowling.
                One
                rolls the ball
                and then one
                and all
          scamper
                merrily
                    down the lane
                        after it.

                    ———

*I*f people were cats
 And lived by the sea,
Seashells and sea glass
 Just wouldn't be
Of very much interest:
 Can't eat them, you see.
I think that instead,
 During sunbathing lulls,
We'd all be collecting
 The horrified gulls.

———

*F*eline catus, office worker,
Contumacious playful lurker,
Hides beneath his desk and waits for
Heedless circumambulators,
Grabs each ankle without warning,
Sends coworkers, startled, soaring
Top the office water cooler!
Feline catus, skulking fooler,
Explain one point didactical:
Why are such jokes called "practical"?

Feline catus, crazed stockbroker,
Races round the stock exchange floor,
Finds his workload is protracted
'Cause he's often too distracted
By those tiny bits of paper
That he's always chasing after.

———

*I*f people, if people, if people
                 were cats
We'd dance along, dance along
                 fences all night,
We'd never, no never, no never
                 go in,
But leap across, leap across
                 rooftops in flight,
And chase after, chase after stars that
                 blow in,
While rolling through, rolling through grass
                 warm and fair,
That summer, oh, summer, had put for
                 us there.
And when on the back porch, our hearts quite
                 gymnastic,
We'd trip the moonlight,
                 the moonlight fantastic.

———

If people were cats,
The kittens, they
Must tiptoe up the stairs,
'Cause shoes are sold in foursomes
Instead of just in pairs.

That's twice as many tennis shoes
        And twice the Birkenstocks,
That's twice as many cowboy boots,
        And twice as many Docs.
That's twice as many clicking heels,
        And anxious tapping toes,
Twice the leaps and jumps and vaults
        Of raging, restless soles.

That's twice as many
Pounding feet
And twice as loud a clatter,
When shoes are sold in foursomes,

And kittens pitter-patter.

————

Driven to

by just the
thought

and shave,

If people were cats,
When it came time for partin',
We'd bury poor Grandma
In the back garden.

Next to the birdbath,
Near flowers bedewed,
Interred with a can
Of her favorite cat food.

Aunt Muffie, Aunt Snowbell—
We'd bury them, too,
And when the time came
That's where we'd put you.

No grim granite gravestones
In bleak cemeteries,
We'd place you beneath
Green trees flecked with cherries.

And on lovely mornings,
The sky bright and blue,
We'd just step out back
To say, "How-do-you-do?"

———

I scream,
You scream,
If people were cats,
We'd all scream

For sardine sherbet,
And mousse made of mice,
For banana slug Jell-O,
And lizards by the slice,

For hummingbird sweetbreads,
And liver-flavored jellies,
For tasty tuna cookies,
To titillate our bellies.

I scream,
You scream,
If people were cats,
We'd all scream

       For snail pie with whipped cream
       And anchovy ice cream.

———

*C*atnip? Catnap?
Catnap? Catnip?
I know the choice is hard.
But if you're going to be a cat,
You're going to have to answer that:
Catnap, catnip.
Which will it be today?

Revelry,
Or reverie,
Well, what do you say?
Recreation, celebration,
Or a long pandiculation,
If you're going to be a cat,
You're going to have to answer that.

Catnip?
Catnap?
High jinks or
Forty winks,
I wish I knew
A way for you
Just simply to
Combine the two,

But you can't have your catnip,
and take a catnap, too.

Catnip, catnap,
Catnap, catnip—
I know the choice is hard.

———

If people were cats, everyone would start **hissing** and jumping
si de wa ys
whenever a dog entered the room.

———

*I*f people were cats, no one would be
    Embarrassed to lounge acrobatically.
Whether dining with friends or a Romanov,
    You'd repose in your chair, half on and half off.

Your head upside down, your limbs in the air,
    Your ears get confused with your derriere.
With cats as with kings, luxuriety
    Dictates all rules of propriety.

(And no one would ever
Dare call you a lout,
For sitting at home
Or out and about
With your tongue emanating
Half out of your mouth.)

———

My dear, I see you've just returned
From San Juan Capistrano,
Where you savored the return
Of all the pretty swallows.

It wasn't hard to guess
That you took that pleasure trip:
There's still a tiny feather
Stuck to your upper lip.

———

If people were cats,
A-rub-a-dub-dub,
We'd all only drink
From the tap of the tub.

Which leaves one to muse
On a theory I'll posit:
Tubs were made for one use—
As the family faucet.

———

*A*ir Meow,
Air Meow,
It flies from Guam
      to Curaçao.
Before our entree of fried goose
(You also have your choice of moose)
We're serving milk and tuna juice
      On lovely Air Meow.

Please don't claw the seats around you
Even if boredom confounds you,
And if you swat our crew, we'll ground you.
      Lovely Air Meow.

Air Meow,
Air Meow,
It flies from Newark
       to Soochow
We'll soar through white clouds cumulus
Just mind your purring stewardpuss
Or else next time you'll take the bus
      Instead of Air Meow.

The use of catnip is forbidden
(Yes, we'll find it if it's hidden)
And *please* stay home if you're flea-bitten.
      Lovely Air Meow.

———

If people were cats
At concerts, I'm sure,
We wouldn't applaud
Instead we'd all purr.

When the great diva finished
Her Carmen with grace,
A communal purr
Would be commonplace.

And when the conductor
Laid down his baton,
The rapturous purring
Would swell on and on.

There's only one problem
We'd come to abhor
When *during* the music
The purrs reached a roar.

"Boo, darling, oh please,"
You'd nudge your sweet spouse,
"Could you keep down the purrs,
Though you love Johann Strauss?
I can't hear a note
Of *Die Fledermaus!*"

———

If people were cats, if people were cats,
Heavens to Betsy, there'd be no more rats,
No mice in the cupboards
No flies on the sill
No moths or odd beetles
　　　Roaming at will,
No roaches tap-dancing
　　　In boudoirs at night
No winged kamikazes
　　　Bumping the light
No diplopods, hexapods,
　　　Omnipods thriving
No green creepy-crawlers
　　　In dank crannies hiving.
If people were cats, the gnats would be nervous,
'Cause eager to pounce and lynx-eyed, and curious,
We'd each be our own
　　　Private pest control service.

———

If Cleopatra had been a cat,
It's she who would've bit the asp,
Then taking hold to firmly clasp it
Would make from it a dandy aspic.

If Nureyev had been a cat,
He would have caused intense delight
By being able on the stage
To *entrechat* ten times his height.

If Torquemada were a cat,
I doubt he would employ the rack;
He'd make poor wretches soon confess
Kneading claws upon their chests.

If Leonardo were a cat,
The *Mona Lisa* legendary
Would have the well-pleased smile of
A cat who swallowed the canary.

If Captain Ahab were a cat
His obsession, I've a hunch,
Would have been with capturing
The world's biggest seafood lunch.

If Audubon had been a cat . . .
Oh, I don't want to think of that.

———

*A*s kittens matured,
If people were cats,
And lost their allure
And acted like brats,
Mothers and fathers
Would look very sad—
Then reach for the phone
To place a want ad:

FREE TO GOOD HOME! One twelve-week-old child, loves to chase insects and run about wild. Has very long tail good for one thing: to be chased round and round like a big piece of string. Free to good home! This scruffy furhead; born in a closet—he's no thoroughbred. At three in the morning, he'll wreck your repose, batting and biting and licking your nose. He eats like a cheetah, except when he sleeps. Free to good home! You can have him—for keeps.

If people were cats,
And kittens were bad,
There's only one option
For poor Mom and Dad,
Just one that will leave
The heart pacified:
Find them new homes
Through a slick classified!

_____

*I*f people were cats, our tails would be
A source of chagrin
        and anxiety.
I'd wager we'd curse
        its length now and then:
"The damn thing is stuck
        in the front door again!"

Or consider a moment
The common lawn mower,
        The motorized fan,
                And the galled moviegoer:
The first grinds it up,
        The next cuts it clean,
                The third gets annoyed
                        When it's blocking the screen.

And riding in cars,
With the windows wide open,
Our parents would chant
That time-honored slogan:

                "Don't stick your tail out too far—
                It might go home in another car!"

                        ———

*I*f people
Were cats
The wild
Would call
More often
Than not
With no warning
At all
A beat deep
Inside you
A rhythm
Provoking
It moves in
Your brain
A stealthy
Invoking

All
At once
You're climbing
The drapes
And watching
Your lover
As if
She were prey
You're chasing
Your tail
You tear
Through the room
For no reason
At all
You're simply
Responding
To some
Primal call

The jungle
The jungle
Your brain
Howls enchained
The walls
Seem absurd
Your sofa
Inane
The carpet
Insane
Beating
Away
In your ears
Hot refrain
The screams of
The jungle
The jungle
Refrain

———

If people were cats, we'd sail in boats
Across an emerald sea
    And use our tails as the mast
    And roam so leisurely
The salt air in our whiskers
The deep beneath our paws
    We'd fish until the sun went down
    Using just our claws
And drift against the sunset
Immune to every fear
    A silhouette against the clouds
    Of big and furry ears
A drifting silhouette against
The sinking, cinnamon sun
    Two cats and four big ears
    Two cats and four big ears
The sea and us in unison
The world and us as one

———

*I*f people were cats, everyone would take a lot more pleasure
in just being here.

———

Author's Note

For their often extraordinary help, both whimsical and pragmatic, I'd like to thank Peter Borland, Richard Donley, Joe Galardi, Danne Hughes, Deirdre Mullane, Charlotte Simmons, and Sam Staggs. Bless you all.